characterfirst education

elementary curriculum
Respect

1 Introduce Respect

This curriculum offers approximately 3 hours of instruction, divided into 3 sections. Each section can be broken into smaller pieces if you prefer short lessons. For additional resources, visit www.CharacterFirstEd.com.

3 WAYS TO BUILD RESPECT:

Educate
Focus on respect for a period of time. Use the lessons in this curriculum to talk about respect and why it matters. Look for ways to emphasize respect during other subjects, such as reading, math, language, history, social studies, science, music, health, and athletics.

Evaluate
Think about daily decisions in the light of good character. Ask yourself and your students, "Is this the right thing to do?" Use the "I Wills" on page 4 as behavioral objectives, and refer to these standards when correcting negative attitudes and behavior.

Celebrate
Catch people doing good and point out the character qualities they demonstrated. Children thrive on sincere encouragement, so don't overlook the little opportunities to praise each day!

© Copyright MMXIV by Character First, a division of Strata Leadership LLC. All rights reserved. No portion of this work may be copied or distributed for personal or commercial use without the publisher's written consent.

Dr. Virginia Smith, president, Character First Ed.
Robert Greenlaw, writer

www.CharacterFirstEd.com
877.357.0001
Printed in the U.S.A.
Item: 04181

978-1-952938-23-8

DEFINE RESPECT
(Discussion, 15 minutes)

Point out and discuss key words in the definition. Review and commit the definition to memory. Use the Respect Character Card (sold separately) to remind or reward students who learn the definition.

Definition: *Treating others with honor and dignity.*

The word *respect* comes from the Latin word *respectus*, meaning "to look back, consider, or regard." When you look at people and consider their worth as human beings, it causes you to treat them with decency, courtesy, and dignity instead of bullying, harassing, or manipulating them.

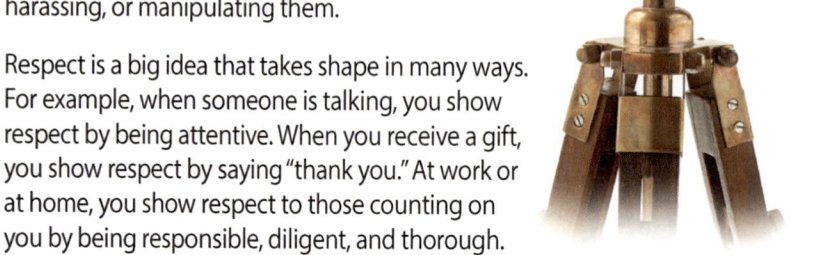

Respect is a big idea that takes shape in many ways. For example, when someone is talking, you show respect by being attentive. When you receive a gift, you show respect by saying "thank you." At work or at home, you show respect to those counting on you by being responsible, diligent, and thorough.

Self-respect means you recognize your own worth as a human being and avoid anything that will damage your mind, body, or integrity. This means you do your best no matter who is watching—because what you do reveals who you are.

Respect does not mean you have to like everyone, and others might not treat you as they should. But respect does not depend on others—it depends on your choice to treat others with the honor and dignity they deserve.

Related concepts:
honor, dignity, courtesy, civility, etiquette, cooperation, deference

Discussion:
- How does it feel when someone shows disrespect?
- How can you respect other students? How can you respect your teachers?
- What is the opposite of respect? (Being rude, mean, hostile.)
- What do you think of this saying? *"Not all disrespect is bullying. But all bullying shows disrespect."*

"I'm not concerned with your liking or disliking me… All I ask is that you respect me as a human being." —Jackie Robinson

MEET AND GREET
(Exploration, 25 minutes)

Teach students how to show courtesy when they meet and greet others, even in different cultures. Role play with students and let them take turns being a "classroom greeter."

One way you show respect is to give people a friendly, courteous greeting. How you do this depends on your situation, but the underlying goal is to treat others with honor and dignity—especially the first time you meet.

The Handshake
- This greeting is common among adults. Extend your hand to the other person for a handshake, grasp firmly (but not too hard), look the person in the eye, and smile. It's okay to shake the hand up and a down a bit, but not too much.

The Wave
- People wave hello and goodbye many different ways. Some waves are big and other waves are small, depending on the situation. When would you use a big wave or a small wave?

The Kiss
- In some cultures, both men and women greet one another with a kiss on one side of the face, then on the other side. Often this is an "air kiss" and not a kiss on the cheek, unless they are close friends or family.

The Salute
- Military service members show respect with a salute. The right arm should extend straight out, and the forearm and hand should point straight toward the eye. (If you are showing children how to salute, you might need to use your left hand so students can easily "mirror" your actions.)

The Hug
- A hug is often used to greet close friends or family. But there are different types of hugs—such as a sideways hug, a gentle hug, a "bear hug," or a long hug.

The Bow
- In some cultures, people greet one another with a bow. People also bow before and after they perform a concert or show.

Verbal Greeting
- Speak clearly and avoid mumbling. Make good eye-contact instead of looking away. Introduce yourself with, "Hello, my name is _____." Use a warm greeting such as, "It's nice to meet you," or "How are you today?"

Respect
Treating others with honor and dignity

SECTION 2: Practice Respect

Teachable Moments

When done correctly, celebrating good character can serve as a teachable moment for other students—not just the one who was "caught being good."

Consider these examples of how to engage other students while honoring those who showed respect:

- "Did you see how Owen let you play the game you wanted to play? That was pretty nice of him to show you respect, wasn't it?"

- "I watched you and Addison have a disagreement a few minutes ago. I appreciate the way you both controlled yourselves and resolved your differences peacefully."

- "Did you notice how Conner asked if his music would bother us? I thought that was very polite of him."

- "I was wondering how we could thank the other students in class for showing good manners at lunch. Do you have any ideas?"

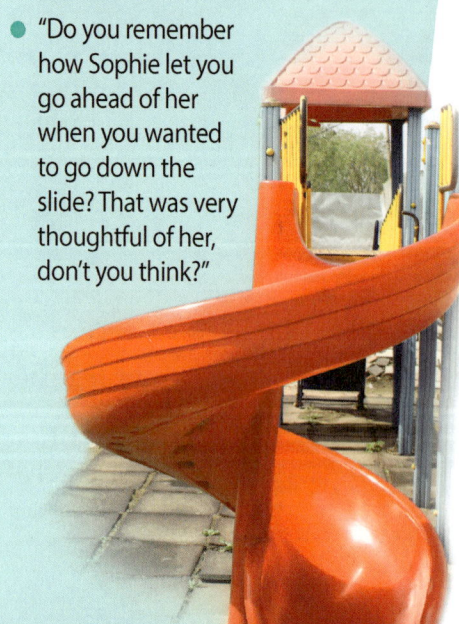

- "Do you remember how Sophie let you go ahead of her when you wanted to go down the slide? That was very thoughtful of her, don't you think?"

I WILL…
(Discussion, 25 minutes)

1. Value others.
People take care of things they value. So if you value other people, you should treat them with kindness and courtesy instead of disrespect or abuse.

- How do you take care of your favorite toy or game?
- How much more important are people—even strangers—than a toy or game? How can you show people you value them?

2. Respect differences.
People are different in many ways, including physical features, personalities, family history, language, culture, beliefs, hobbies, and talents. Try to learn from others instead of expecting them to be the same as you.

- What would the world be like if everyone was the same?
- How can you disagree with someone and still show respect?

3. Use good manners.
Show respect by opening doors for others, using good table manners, using appropriate language, and respecting other people's belongings.

- How can you show good manners at meal time?
- Why should you avoid using crude, vulgar, hateful, and offensive language?

4. Not bully or harass others.
Do not threaten or hurt others in order to get what you want. Treat everyone with respect, and protect those who cannot protect themselves.

- Why is it wrong to bully others in order to get your way?
- Who can you ask for help if you feel threatened or afraid?
- Just because someone disagrees with you or is inconsiderate doesn't make that person a bully. How can you tell the difference?

5. Treat people the way I want to be treated.
This is often called "The Golden Rule" because it helps you figure out how to treat others with honor, dignity, love, kindness, and respect.

- What should you do if someone is rude or mean to you? What would you want someone to do if *you* were the one being unkind?

WORD FILTER
(Project, 25 minutes)

Encourage students to "filter" their words and speak respectfully to one another.

Words are extremely powerful. With words you can build someone up or tear someone down. Sometimes you need to "filter" your words in order to speak respectfully instead of saying whatever comes to mind.

Make a visual reminder of this by stapling a coffee filter to a sheet of paper. Write "I Will Show Respect" at the top of the page, and the definition of respect at the bottom.

Cut another piece of paper into strips and write encouraging words or "Super Sayings" on each piece. Keep the pieces in place by stapling them to the coffee filter.

Supplies: paper, coffee filters, stapler, scissors, markers; download "Super Sayings" from www.CharacterFirstEd.com

Super Sayings
— I Will Show Respect! —

- "Have a good day!"
- "You're doing great!"
- "Thank you so much!"
- "Super job!"
- "You're a great friend!"
- "Keep up the good work!"
- "Nice to see you."
- "We're behind you all the way!"
- "Let me know if I can help."

MY DECLARATION
(Project, 25 minutes)

Use a bit of American history to emphasize that everyone should be treated with dignity and respect.

The *Declaration of Independence* is considered the "birth certificate" of the United States of America. It's opening lines include these famous words: "We hold these truths to be self-evident, that all men are created equal, that they are endowed by their Creator with certain unalienable Rights, that among these are Life, Liberty, and the pursuit of Happiness."

This reminds us that everyone deserves dignity and respect because of their worth as a human being. Help students remember these words by writing them on the board for students to copy onto sheets of blank or parchment paper. You might also create a bulletin board using this historical theme.

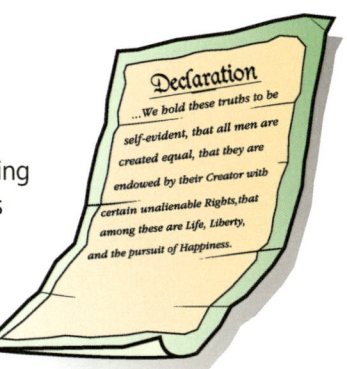

Supplies: blank or parchment paper, pens or markers

Points to Ponder:
- Showing respect doesn't mean you agree with everyone. But it does mean you value others because of their worth as a human being.
- Respect is something you give whether someone is young or old, rich or poor, male or female, or any other difference.
- Use this lesson as a history prompt. Study the Declaration of Independence or the lives of its 56 signers.

RESPECT POEM
(Literacy Connection, 15 minutes)

Teach this poem as a way to memorize the five "I Wills." Watch the video at www.CharacterFirstEd.com.

I will value other people and I never will forget,
That even though we're different, I can still show you respect.

I will always use good manners. I'll be careful what I say.
I will treat others with dignity in how I live each day.

My character is what will make a leader out of me.
So next time through, let's say it more ENTHUSIASTICALLY!

SECTION 3 Respect in Real Life

Charles Young

One evening, Charles and a friend played soldiers in his bedroom. "Attention!" Charles shouted loudly. Then Charles heard a knock on the front door and his mother talking to a friend. "We better be quiet," Charles said. "Mother wouldn't want us to make a bunch of noise now that we have company around."

When the visitor left, Charles' mom walked into the room. "How respectful of you to notice I had company," she said. "You boys will make fine gentlemen."

Charles attended West Point Military Academy and joined the US Army where he served for 33 years. On one assignment, he went to the African country of Liberia to gather intelligence and build relationships with the local people.

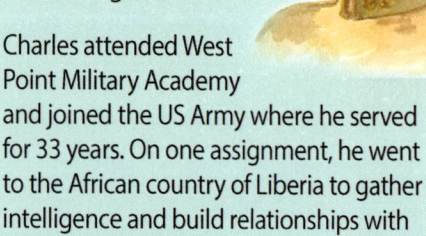

Charles quickly discovered he and the Liberians had many differences. But he respected their culture and tried to make new friends. He reported any problems he found to Liberia's leaders, and he even kept a civil war from breaking out.

By the time Charles returned to the United States, he was a national hero in Liberia. "It has been a pleasure," said the Liberian President, "to know such a true and noble gentleman."

Read more about Charles Young at www.CharacterFirstEd.com.

The timber wolf is a recognized symbol of freedom and independence. However, the strength of a wolf pack is not in a single individual, but in the ability of the whole pack to live and work together in harmony.

THE TIMBER WOLF
(Story, 15 minutes)

Two large timber wolves met on an empty trail. They both stood their ground and stared at each other. Because wolves are so strong and powerful, a fight of any kind would bring certain harm to one wolf or the other.

Tension built as the two wolves growled at each other. The hair on their necks stood on end, and their tails pointed straight up. Each wolf lowered its head and crept closer toward the other. They snarled and showed their sharp fangs. A fight seemed almost certain.

But suddenly, one wolf stopped. It paused for just a moment and lifted its head. Its tail relaxed, and the hair on its neck smoothed out as if an invisible comb had brushed across its back. The wolf stepped cautiously to one side.

Almost instantly, the second wolf relaxed. It also stepped back. Both wolves kept their eyes fixed on one another as the growls quieted to a whisper. Slowly and carefully, each wolf side-stepped its way past the other. A fight just wasn't worth the trouble and pain it would cause. They chose to show respect and go their separate ways in peace.

Stick Together
Respect is essential for wolves to keep the peace among themselves. With 5 to 10 wolves in a pack, any fighting among them weakens their ability to defend themselves and hunt for food. Being rude, mean, or selfish leads to fights, and wolves that fight don't last very long.

Respect is also important for people to get along with one another. It helps us keep the peace with our classmates, neighbors, family members, and friends.

Let Others Go First
When wolves meet on a trail, they often show their teeth and growl. But usually one wolf steps aside to let the other pass. Wolves do this based on a ranking system that shows who is in charge. For example, wolf B will step aside for wolf A, and wolf C will yield to wolves A and B. Wolf D will defer to A, B, and C.

One way you can show respect is to let others go first. This doesn't mean you are weaker or less important—it means you are courteous, thoughtful, and unselfish.

Give Some Space

Have you ever heard a wolf howl at night? It can sound frightening. But sometimes wolves howl in order to show respect to one another.

When a wolf enters new territory, it howls to see if other wolves have already claimed that area. If the wolves that live there howl back, the new wolf looks for another place to live. Wolves do this in order to give each other space and respect the boundaries between them.

People also have boundaries. That's why you don't enter someone else's home without permission, or dig through someone's backpack or notebook, or play your music so loud that it bothers people around you. Be aware of your surroundings and give people the space they need.

Calm the Situation

When tensions rise, wolves can make the situation better or worse based on how they respond. For example, an angry wolf sticks its tail straight out, which means it is asking for a fight. A scared wolf tucks its tail between its legs and hides. A happy wolf waves its tail back and forth, which irritates the angry wolf. But a peaceful wolf points its tail down, stays calm, and backs up a few steps in order to avoid a needless fight.

When others are upset, don't make the problem worse by yelling back, calling names, threatening them, laughing it off, or being afraid. Stay calm, back off a little, choose your words carefully, and get help from someone you trust. You don't have to agree with everyone and you don't have to be best friends—but you *do* need to show respect.

Keep the peace by showing respect, and you'll make life better for everyone.

A WOLF'S TAIL
(Project, 25 minutes)

Help students make their own timber wolves. Download a template at www.CharacterFirstEd.com.

Have students cut out the shape of a wolf. Attach ears and a tail with brass fasteners so they can move, like a wolf that uses its body language to show respect to other wolves. Write the five "I Wills" for respect on the back of the wolf.

Watch a video of the Timber Wolf Story at www.CharacterFirstEd.com

Family Connection

OVERVIEW: **Everyone has worth and dignity as a human being,** regardless of being young or old, rich or poor, male or female, or any other difference. This is why you should treat others with honor, dignity, and courtesy instead of bullying, harassing, or manipulating in order to get what you want. Even when you disagree with others or have to part ways, you can still treat them with the dignity and respect they deserve.

Respect

Definition: Treating others with honor and dignity

I WILL...
- ❏ Value others.
- ❏ Respect differences.
- ❏ Use good manners.
- ❏ Not bully or harass others.
- ❏ Treat people the way I want to be treated.

The Timber Wolf shows respect to other wolves through a variety of signs and motions. This behavior helps a wolf pack live and work together in harmony.

CHARACTER QUIZ:

1. Why should you treat others with respect? _____

2. Imagine if everyone was mean, harsh, rude, and disrespectful. What kind of a world would that be?
   _____

3. Being respectful means you: **a.** agree with everyone. **b.** never do what you want. **c.** treat others the way you want to be treated.

4. A respectful person tries to live peacefully with others: YES? or NO?

5. What are some good manners you can show at meal time, at the store, or at school?
   _____

This page may be copied and distributed for educational use.
© Copyright MMXIV by Character First. 877.357.0001 www.CharacterFirstEd.com

cf character first education

Lightning Source UK Ltd.
Milton Keynes UK
UKRC010224260620
365593UK00003B/41